The Artful Cat

by Salvador

PRIMA

First published by Virgin Publishing in 1993
This edition published by Prima Publishing in 1994

Salvador.
        The artful cat / by Salvador.
            p.   cm.
        ISBN 1-55958-585-4
        1. Cats–Caricatures and cartoons. 2. English wit and humor,
    Pictorial.   I. Title.
    NC1479.S25A4   1994
    741.5′942–dc20
                                                            94-20294
                                                            CIP

Design and layout by Stan Eales

Typeset by Phoenix Photosetting, Chatham, Kent

Printed and bound by Proost, Belgium

Rodin tries to out-stare his cat

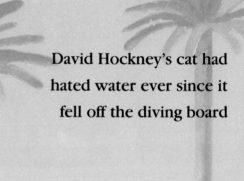

David Hockney's cat had
hated water ever since it
fell off the diving board

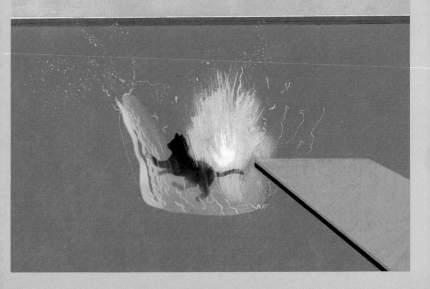

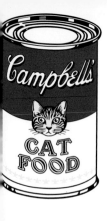

Andy Warhol took a small break from painting soup cans

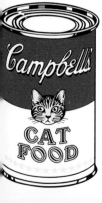

Mrs Seurat soon had the whole
room full of flea powder

Being kicked was a constant problem for Toulouse-Lautrec's cat

Chagall's cat suddenly wished

that he'd never ever sipped

any of that alcohol stuff

Edvard Munch was having
problems toilet-training
his kitten

And yet Rousseau had the cheek to complain when the cat laid around and slept all day

The RSPCA were horrified
at what Francis Bacon had
done to his cat

The Lichtensteins' cat
was driving them dotty

The cat knew
how to wake
Dali when it
was time to
be fed

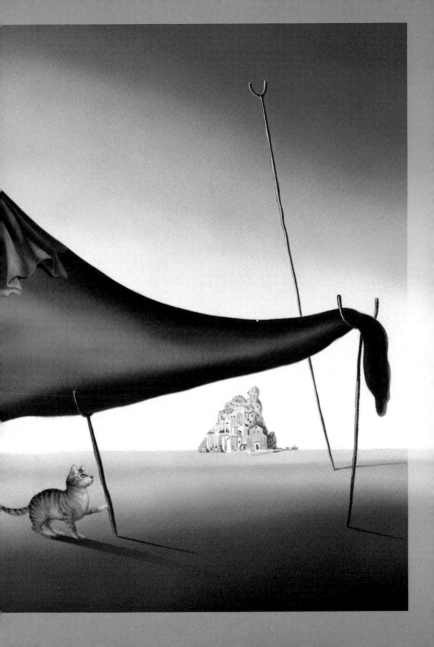

Those cursed waterlilies
were obscuring Monet's
cat's view of the goldfish

Matisse's cat got flattened
on the motorway at night

What de Chirico's cat hated
worse than going on holiday,
was being forgotten at
the train station

Bridget Riley's cat had
some unusual fur markings

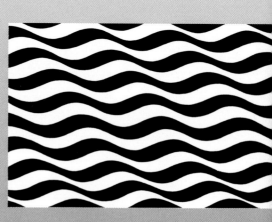

Magritte's cat suddenly regretted
everything that it had ever done
to budgies and goldfish

"No you little swine,
you'll claw my legs
to bits if you climb
up on my lap"

Jackson Pollock
hadn't realised
that his cat had
been sleeping
on his canvas

Mondrian's cat
had trouble
finding the
cat flap

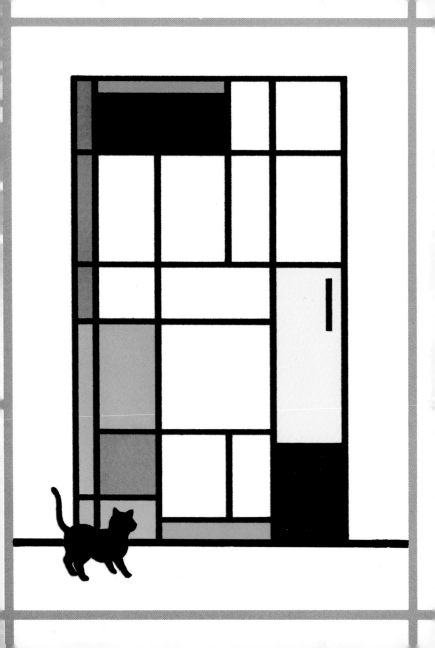

The cat *would* have to fall
asleep just when Mrs Whistler
needed to go to the toilet

Picasso always had problems getting his tom cat to eat cheap cat food

Aubrey Beardsley, being a vegetarian, hated cutting up fresh meat for the cat's dinner

It was annoying how the
cat started clawing the
duvet as soon as the Klimts
started humping

Giacometti was as stingy
with his cat's food as
he was with his own